Compositions
for Baroque Lute

Matthew Leigh EMBLETON (b1978)

Copyright ©2020 Matthew Leigh Embleton. All rights reserved.

Compositions for Baroque Lute

Op 01 Journey in d-minor...4
Op 02 Nocturnes in d-minor and e-minor 7
Op 03 From Depth in a-minor..9
Op 04 Nocturnes in f-minor and g-minor 10
Op 05 Small Floating Crafts in c-minor...13
Op 06 Journey in a-minor...18
Op 07 Journey in c-minor...22
Op 08 Nocturne in c-minor...28
Op 09 Tasmanian Lake d-minor...30
Op 10 Extransience in d-minor..32
Op 11 Victoria Park, December 2005 in e-minor (Version 1)...33
Op 11 Victoria Park, December 2005 in e-minor (Version 2)...34
Op 12 Late Night Sky in g-minor 35
Op 13 Introduction in g-minor...36

Acknowledgments

Thanks to Susan King, David Van Ooijen, Stuart Walsh, Steve Metcalfe, and Wezi Elliot for their feedback, collaboration, support, and encouragement.

Thanks to Luke Emmett and Christopher Goodwin, Stewart McCoy, Christopher Wilson, Shirley Rumsey, Richard Mackenzie, Taro Takeuchi, Zak Ozmo, Lynda Sayce, Brian Wright, Stephanie Feeney, Denys Stephens, and The Lute Society (https://www.lutesociety.org/)

Thanks to Matteo Simone, Francesco Tribioli, Gian Luca Lastraioli, Giorgio Ferraris, Franco Fois, Massimo Marchese, and the Società del Liuto (http://societadelliuto.it/)

Thanks to Catherine Liddell, Dan Larson, Nancy Carlin, and The Lute Society of America (http://lutesocietyofamerica.org/)

Thanks to the special people in my life who have supported and encouraged me in my work. Thank you for believing in me. You know who you are.

Matthew Leigh Embleton (b1978) — Compositions for Baroque Lute

Op 01 Journey in d-minor

01 Introduction, *piano con affetto*

©2012, 2013, 2015, and 2020 Matthew Leigh Embleton

Matthew Leigh Embleton (b1978) — Compositions for Baroque Lute

02 The Pursuit, *con affetto e un poco agitato*

©2012, 2013, 2015, and 2020 Matthew Leigh Embleton

Matthew Leigh Embleton (b1978) — Compositions for Baroque Lute

03 Looking Skyward, *con larghezza*

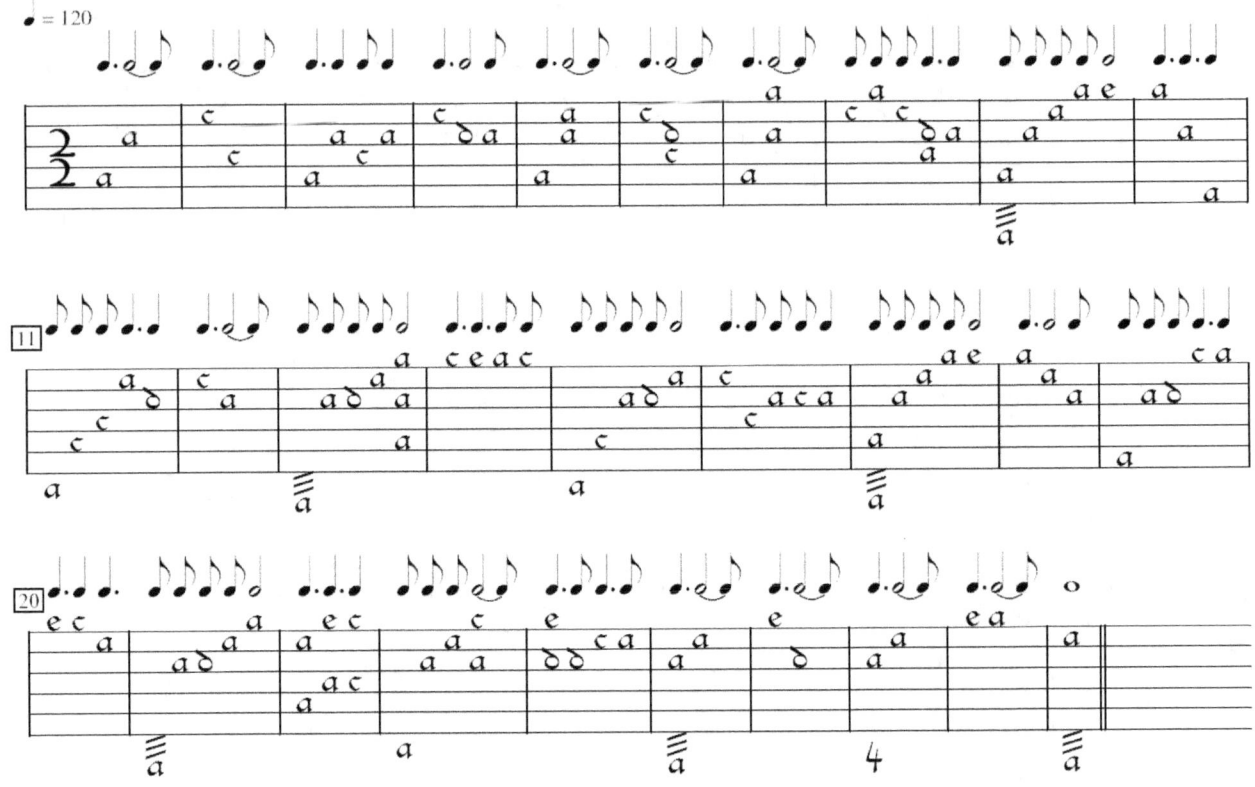

©2012, 2013, 2015, and 2020 Matthew Leigh Embleton

Matthew Leigh Embleton (b1978) — Compositions for Baroque Lute

Op 02 Nocturnes in d-minor and e-minor

01 Nocturne in d-minor, *piano molto e cantabile*

©2012, 2013, 2015, and 2020 Matthew Leigh Embleton

Matthew Leigh Embleton (b1978) Compositions for Baroque Lute

02 Nocturne in e-minor, *piano molto e cantabile*

©2012, 2013, 2015, and 2020 Matthew Leigh Embleton

Matthew Leigh Embleton (b1978) — Compositions for Baroque Lute

Op 03 From Depth in a-minor

Piano molto e penseroso

©2012, 2013, 2015, and 2020 Matthew Leigh Embleton

Op 04 Nocturnes in f-minor and g-minor

01 Nocturne in f-minor, *piano molto e cantabile*

©2012, 2013, 2015, and 2020 Matthew Leigh Embleton

Matthew Leigh Embleton (b1978) — Compositions for Baroque Lute

02 Nocturne in g-minor (Version 1), *piano molto e cantabile*

©2012, 2013, 2015, and 2020 Matthew Leigh Embleton

Matthew Leigh Embleton (b1978) — Compositions for Baroque Lute

02 Nocturne in g-minor (Version 2), *piano molto e cantabile*

Matthew Leigh Embleton (b1978) — Compositions for Baroque Lute

Op 05 Small Floating Crafts in c-minor

01 Introduction, *con rubato e improvvisazione*

©2012, 2013, 2015, and 2020 Matthew Leigh Embleton

Matthew Leigh Embleton (b1978) — Compositions for Baroque Lute

02 Interlude, *con rubato e improvvisazione*

Matthew Leigh Embleton (b1978) — Compositions for Baroque Lute

©2012, 2013, 2015, and 2020 Matthew Leigh Embleton

Matthew Leigh Embleton (b1978) — Compositions for Baroque Lute

03 Conclusion, *con rubato e improvvisazione*

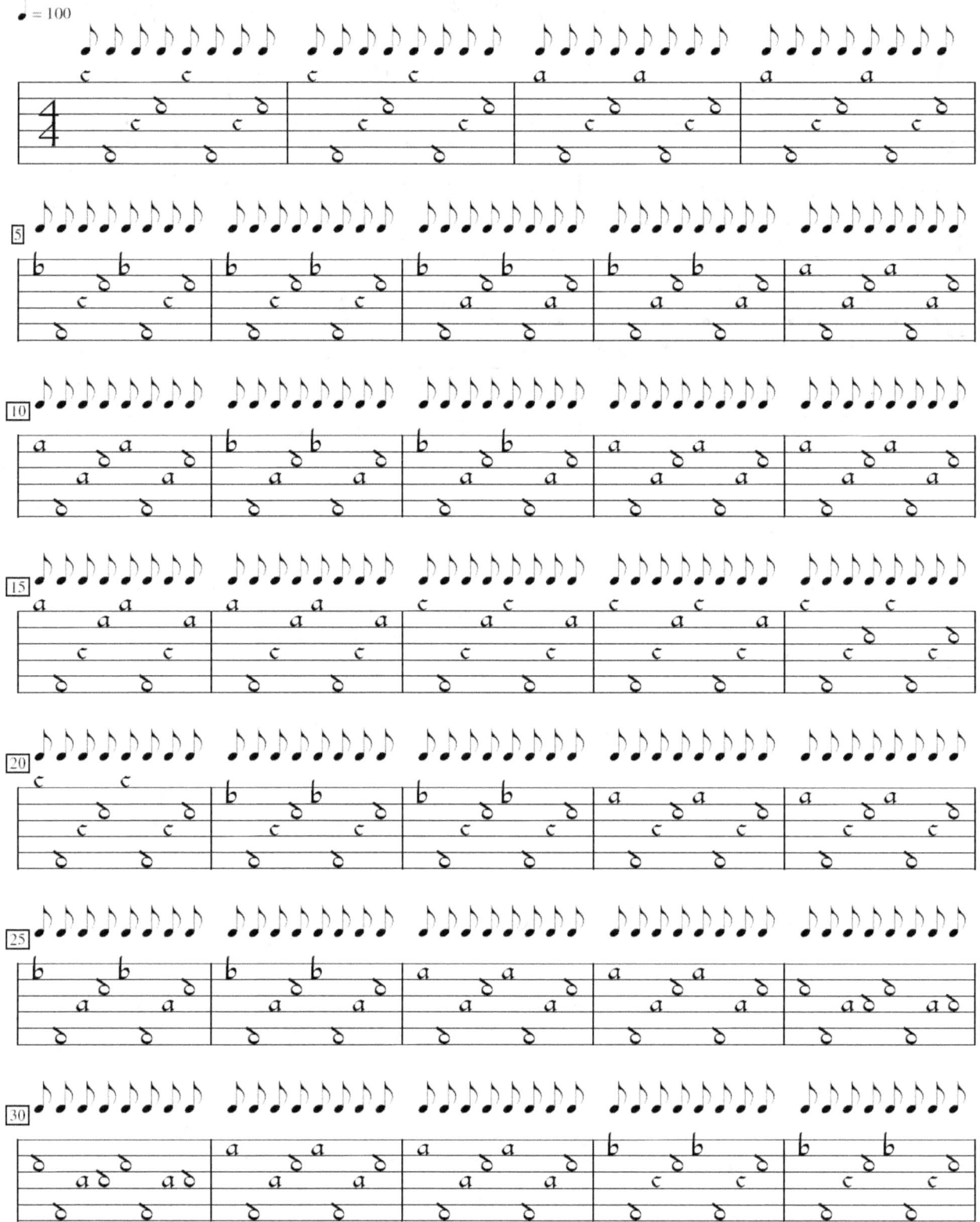

©2012, 2013, 2015, and 2020 Matthew Leigh Embleton

Matthew Leigh Embleton (b1978) — Compositions for Baroque Lute

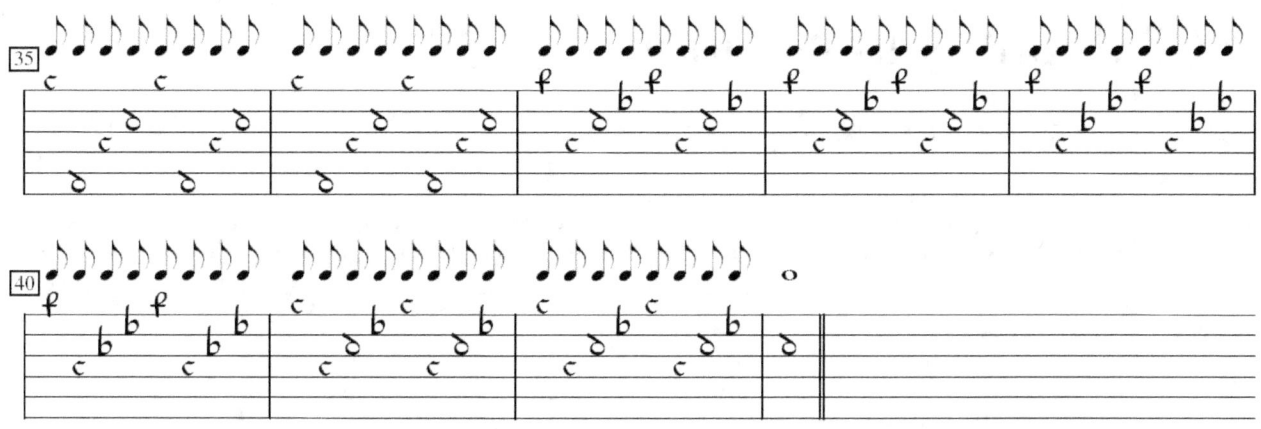

Matthew Leigh Embleton (b1978) — Compositions for Baroque Lute

Op 06 Journey in a-minor

01 Arpeggiata, *adagio andante e piano*

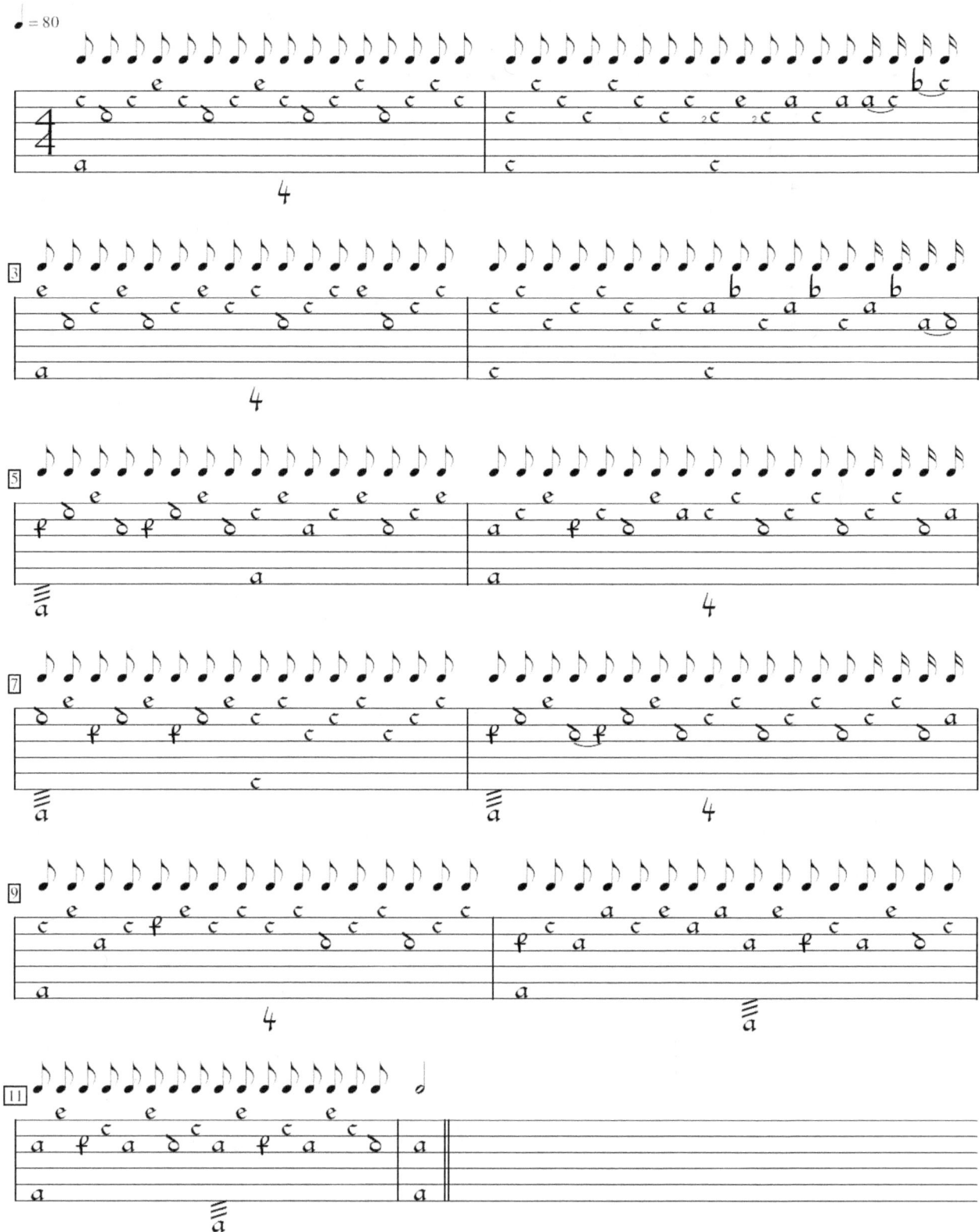

©2012, 2013, 2015, and 2020 Matthew Leigh Embleton

Matthew Leigh Embleton (b1978) — Compositions for Baroque Lute

02 Cloud Level (Version 1), *piano molto e penseroso*

Matthew Leigh Embleton (b1978) Compositions for Baroque Lute

02 Cloud Level (Version 2), *piano molto e penseroso*

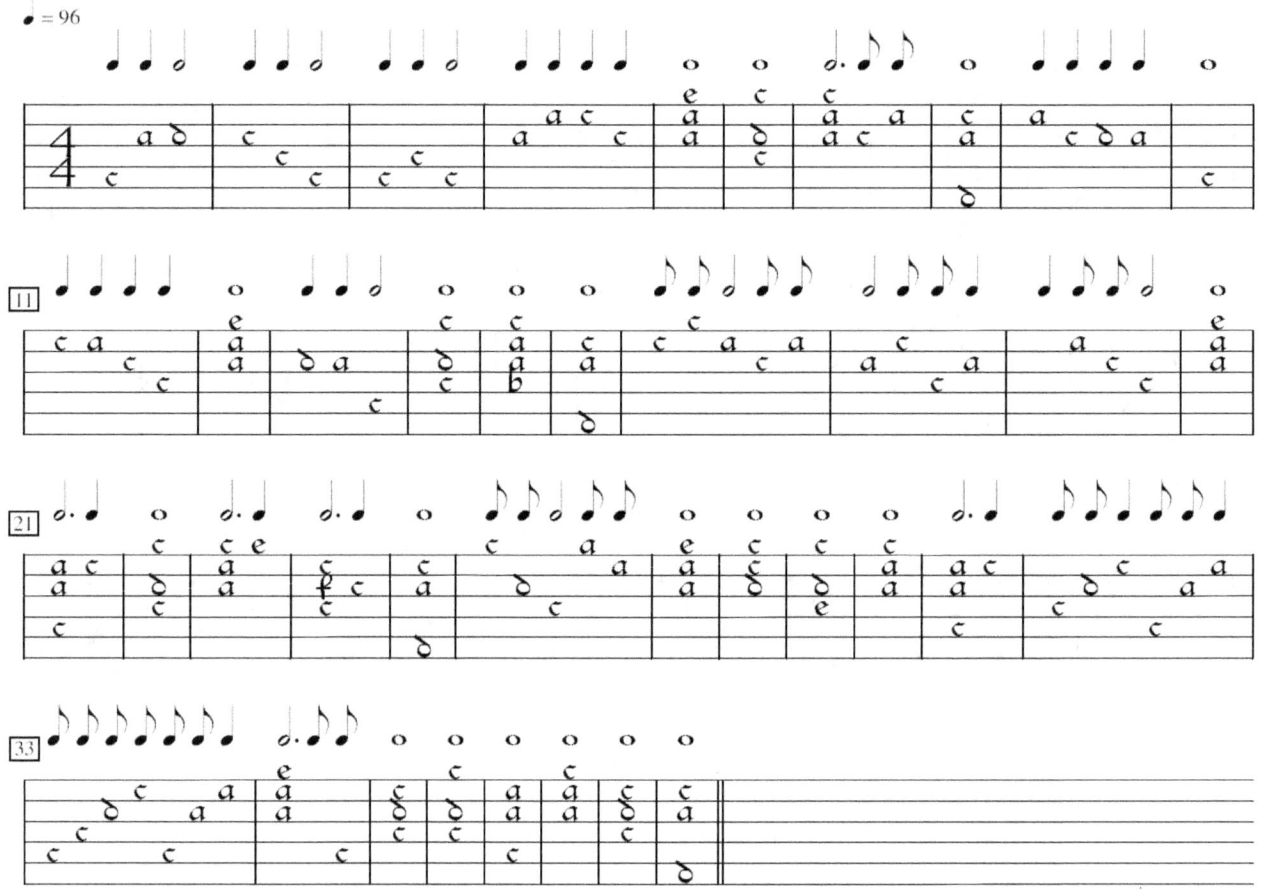

©2012, 2013, 2015, and 2020 Matthew Leigh Embleton

Matthew Leigh Embleton (b1978) — Compositions for Baroque Lute

03 Eternal Recurrence, *piano molto con affetuoso*

©2012, 2013, 2015, and 2020 Matthew Leigh Embleton

Matthew Leigh Embleton (b1978) — Compositions for Baroque Lute

Op 07 Journey in c-minor

01 Introduction, *andante*

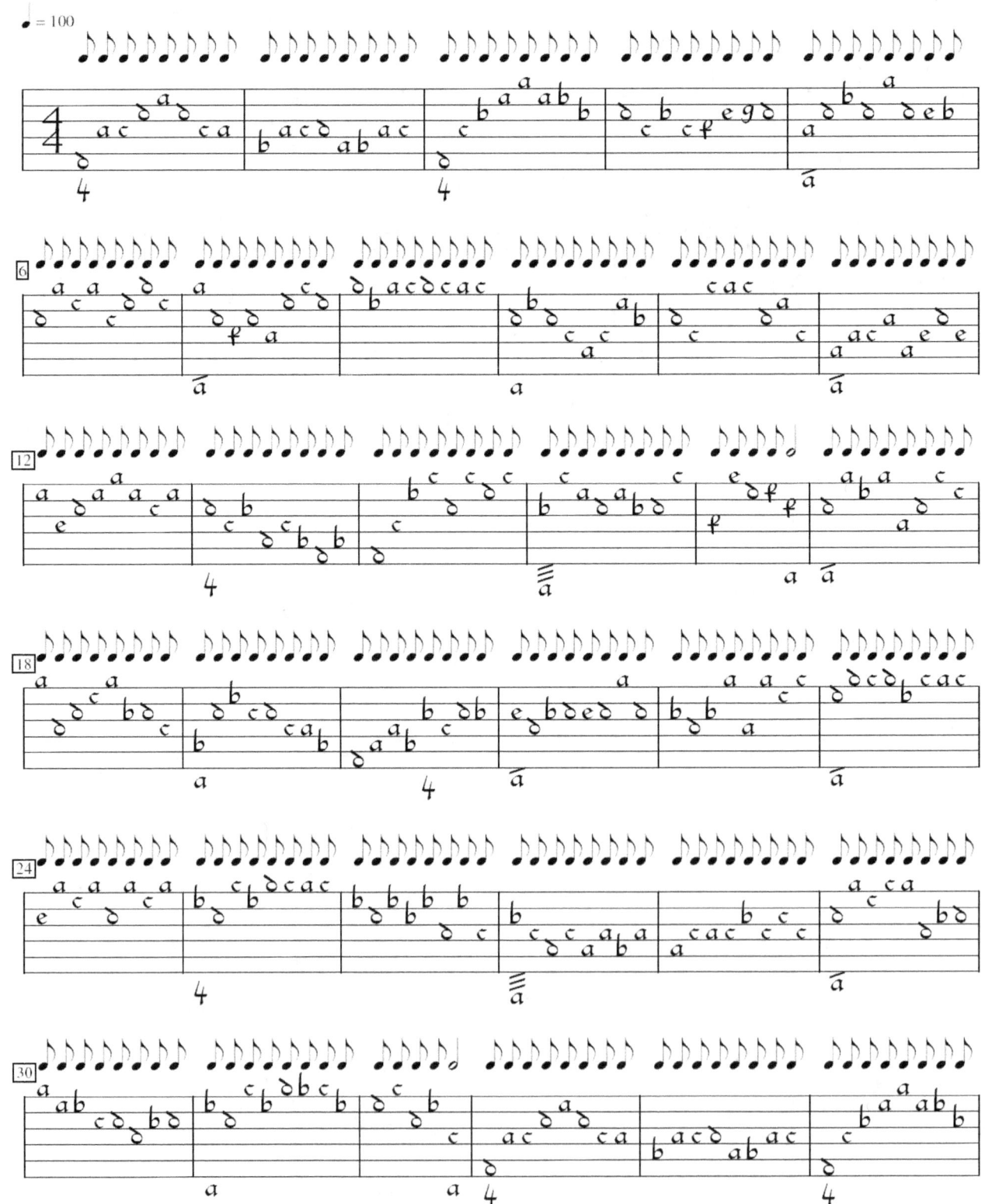

©2012, 2013, 2015, and 2020 Matthew Leigh Embleton

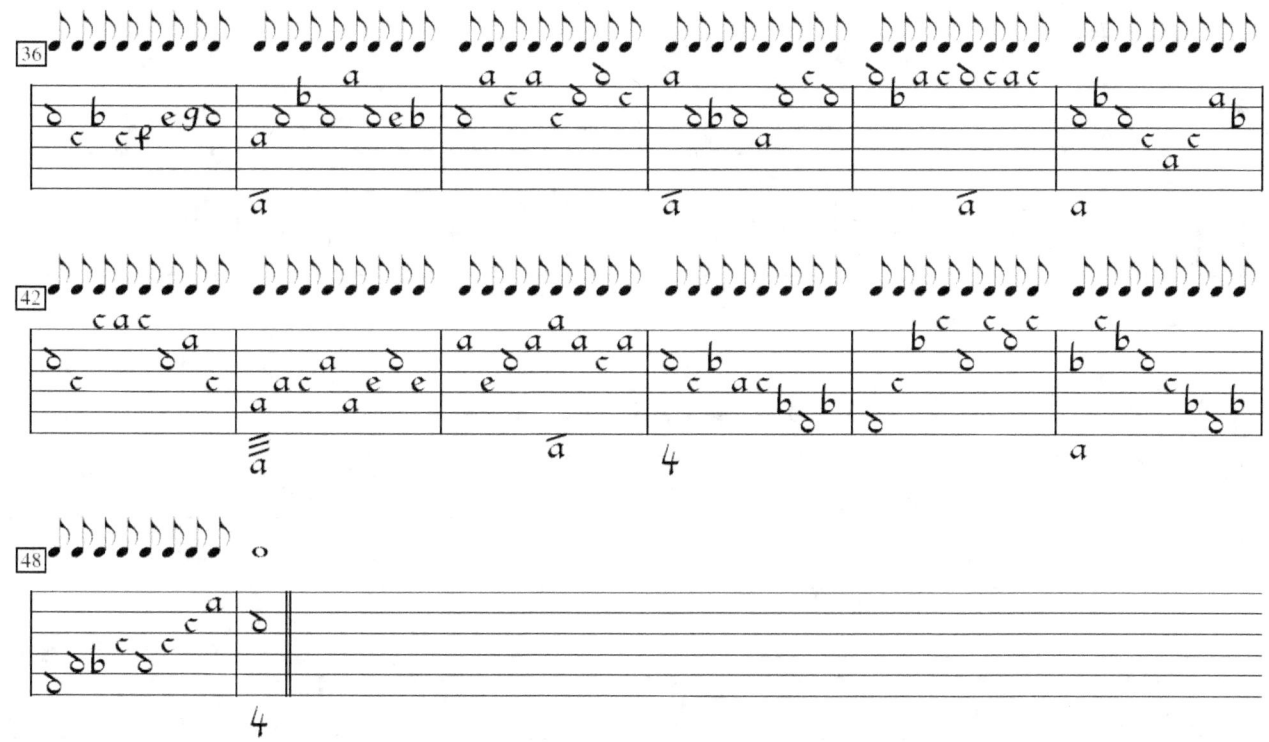

Matthew Leigh Embleton (b1978) — Compositions for Baroque Lute

02 Interlude, *adagio*

©2012, 2013, 2015, and 2020 Matthew Leigh Embleton

Matthew Leigh Embleton (b1978) — Compositions for Baroque Lute

03 Conclusion, *allegro*

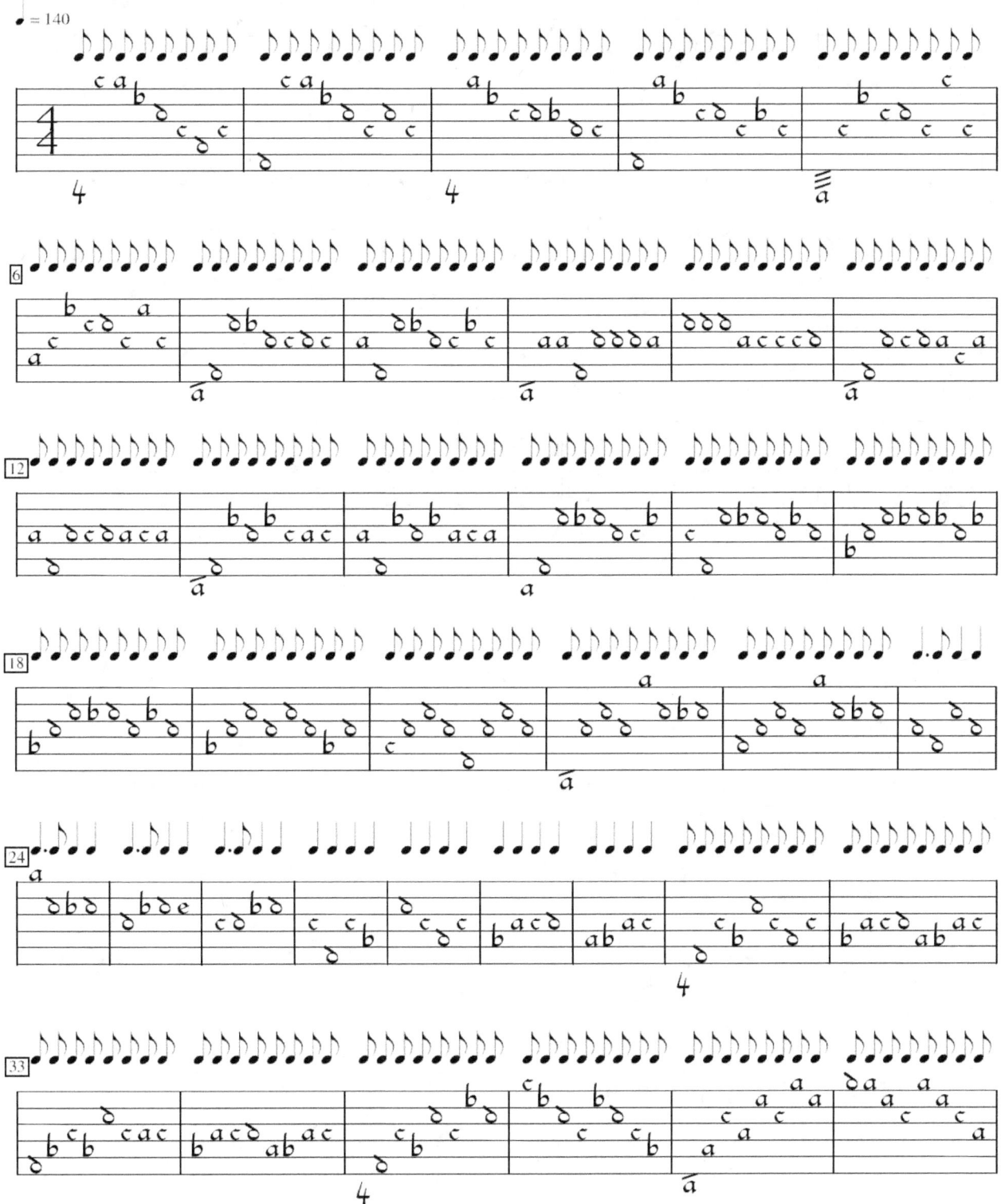

©2012, 2013, 2015, and 2020 Matthew Leigh Embleton

Matthew Leigh Embleton (b1978) — Compositions for Baroque Lute

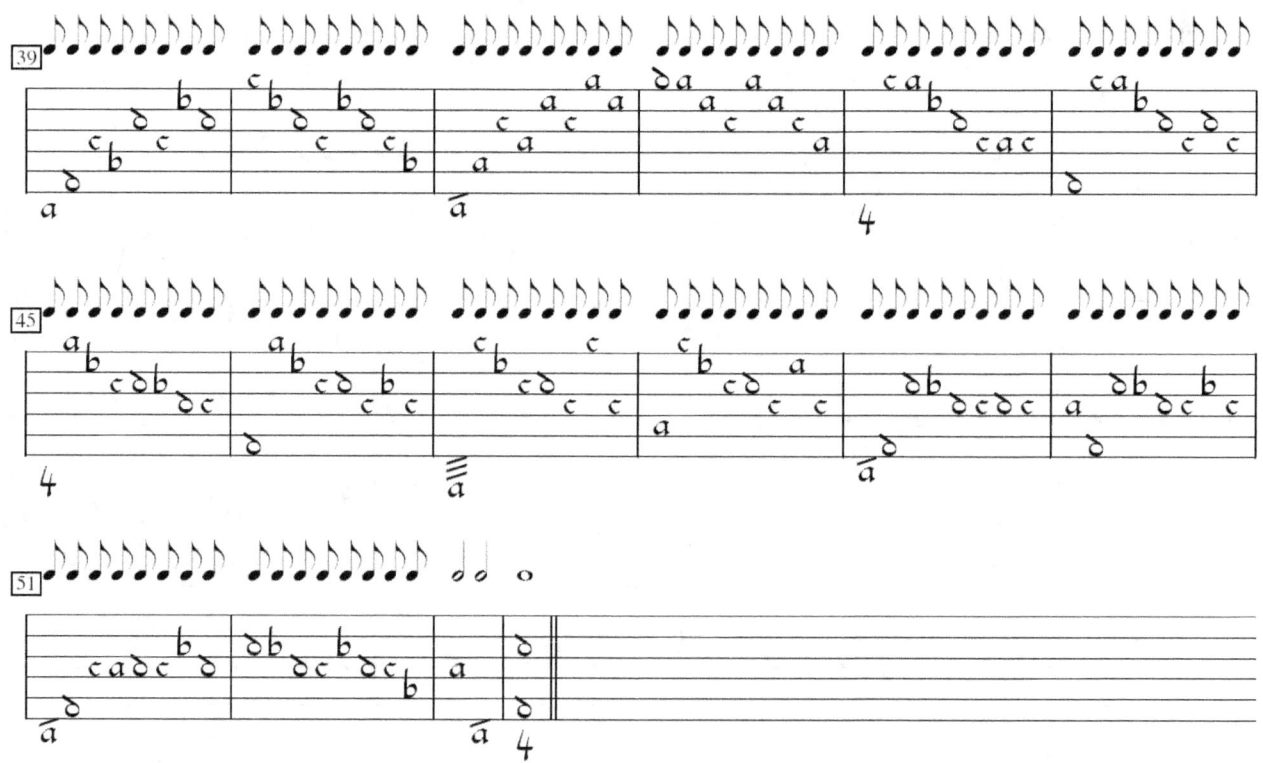

Matthew Leigh Embleton (b1978) — Compositions for Baroque Lute

Op 08 Nocturne in c-minor

Piano molto e cantabile

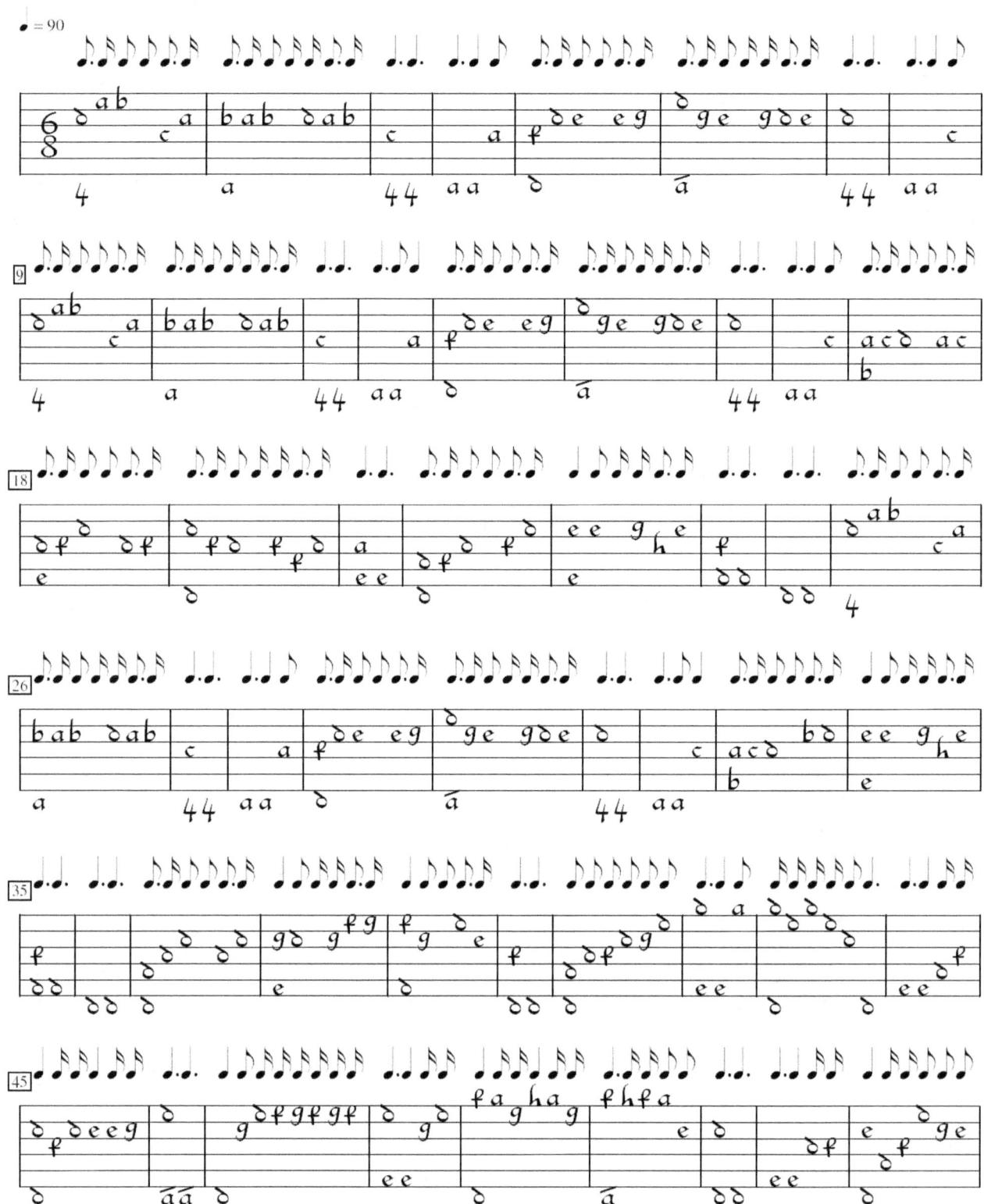

©2012, 2013, 2015, and 2020 Matthew Leigh Embleton

Matthew Leigh Embleton (b1978) — Compositions for Baroque Lute

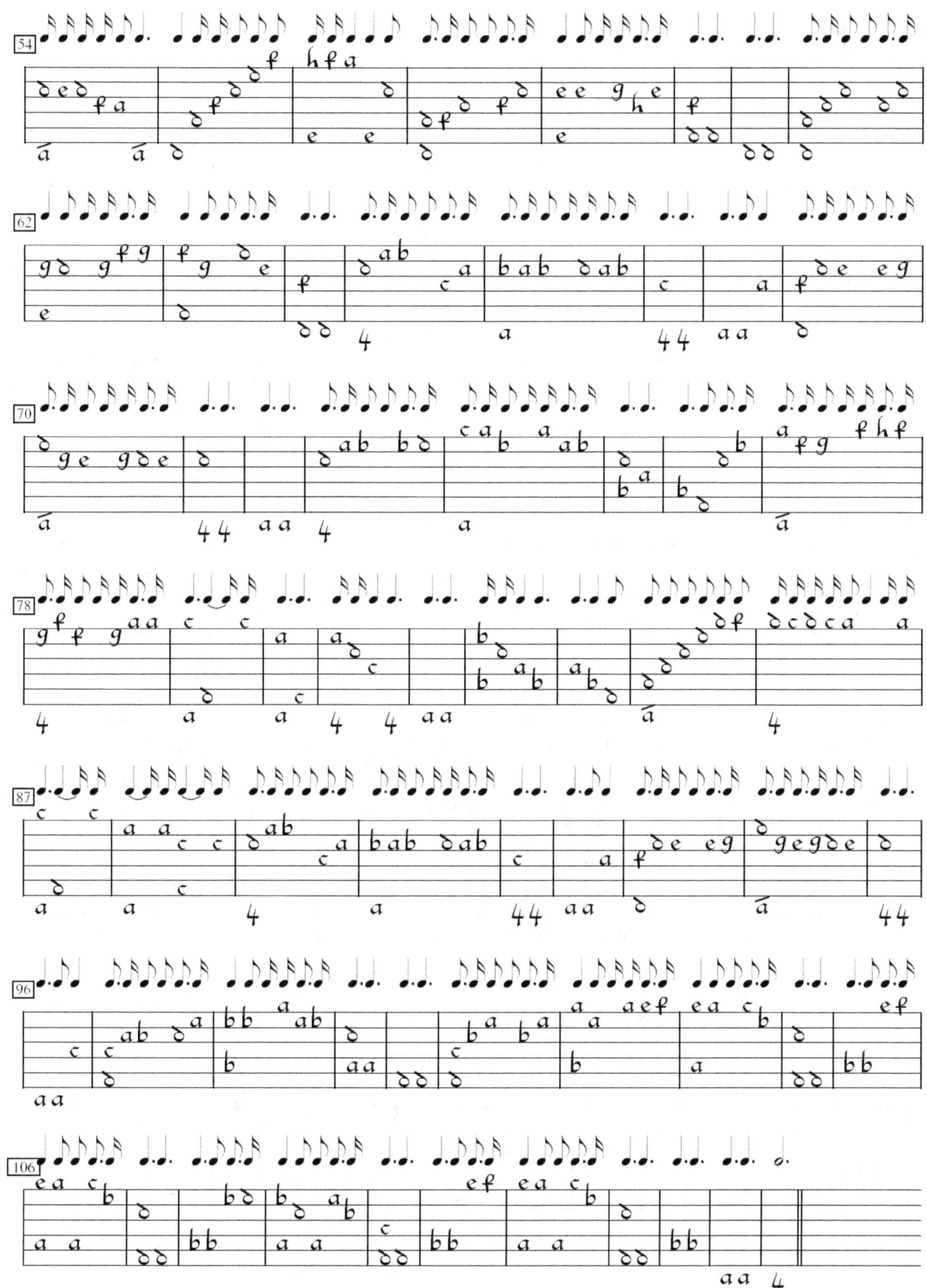

©2012, 2013, 2015, and 2020 Matthew Leigh Embleton

Matthew Leigh Embleton (b1978) — Compositions for Baroque Lute

Op 09 Tasmanian Lake d-minor

Piano molto e penseroso

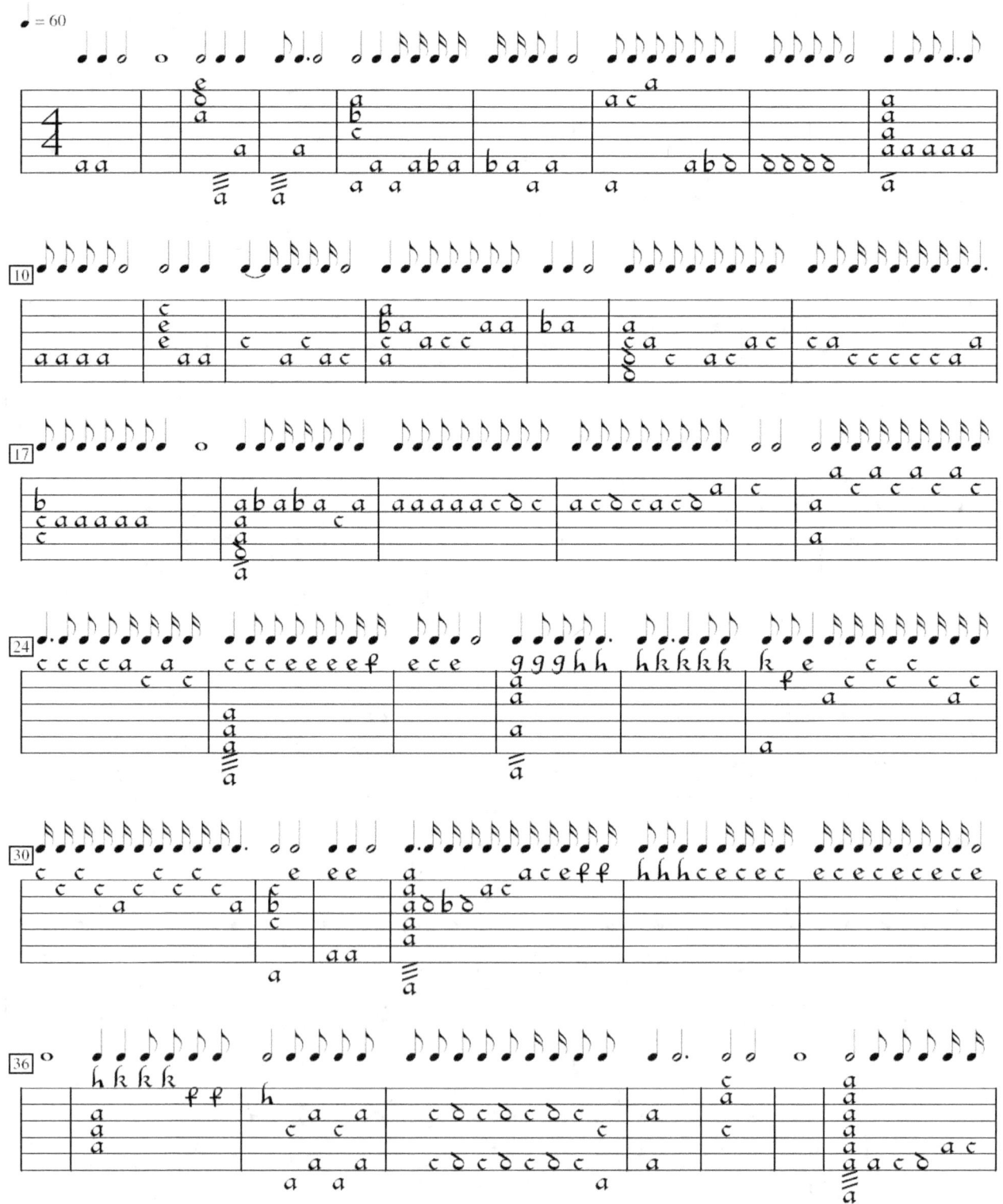

©2012, 2013, 2015, and 2020 Matthew Leigh Embleton

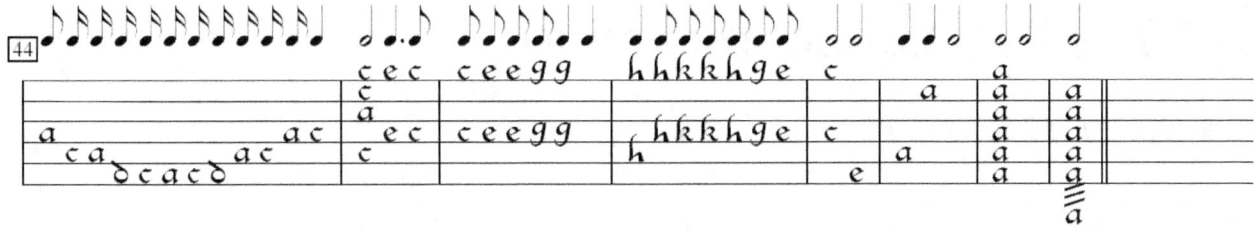

Matthew Leigh Embleton (b1978) — Compositions for Baroque Lute

Op 10 Extransience in d-minor

Affrettando con poco agitato

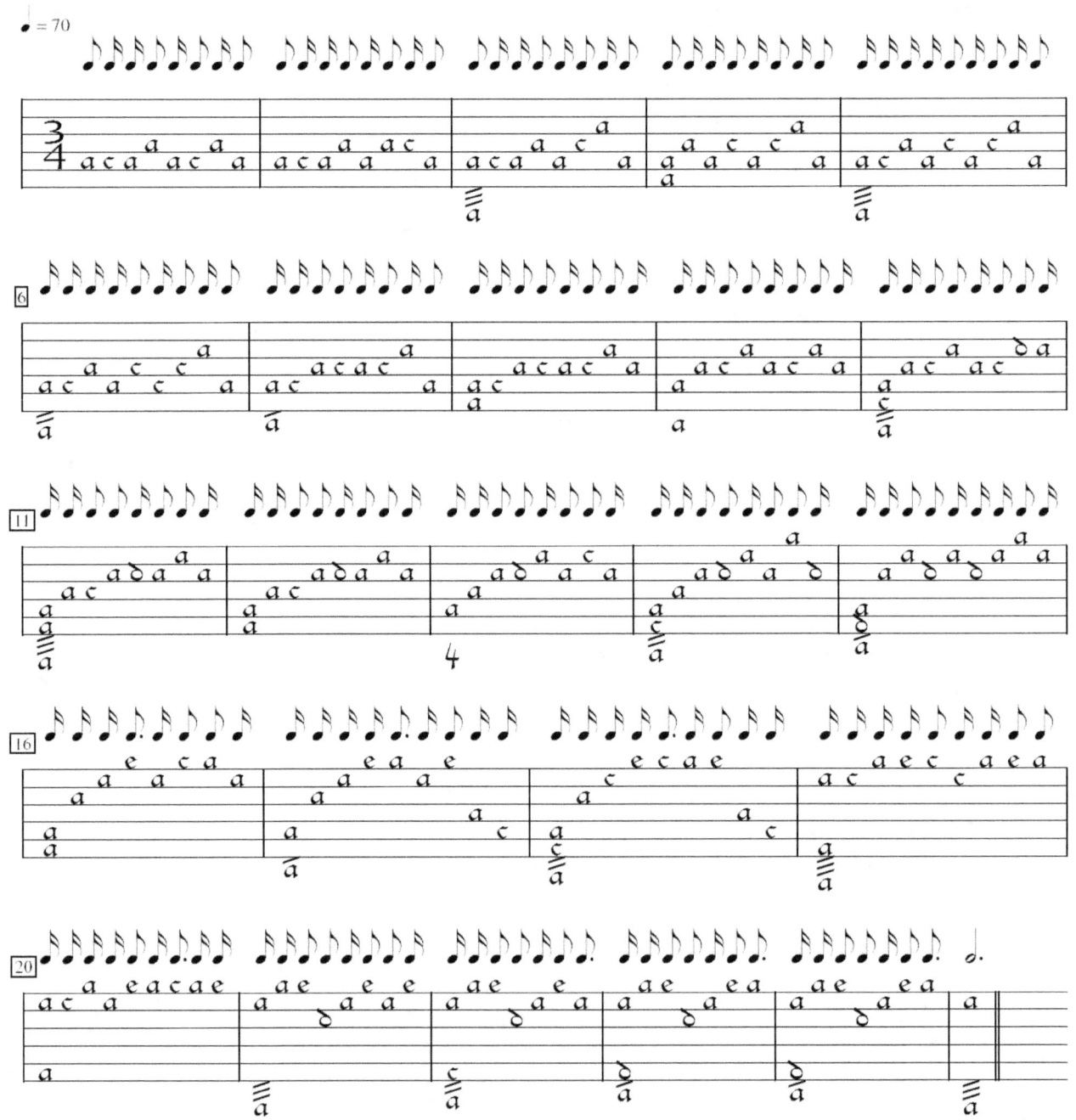

©2012, 2013, 2015, and 2020 Matthew Leigh Embleton

Op 11 Victoria Park, December 2005 in e-minor (Version 1)

Piano molto e penseroso

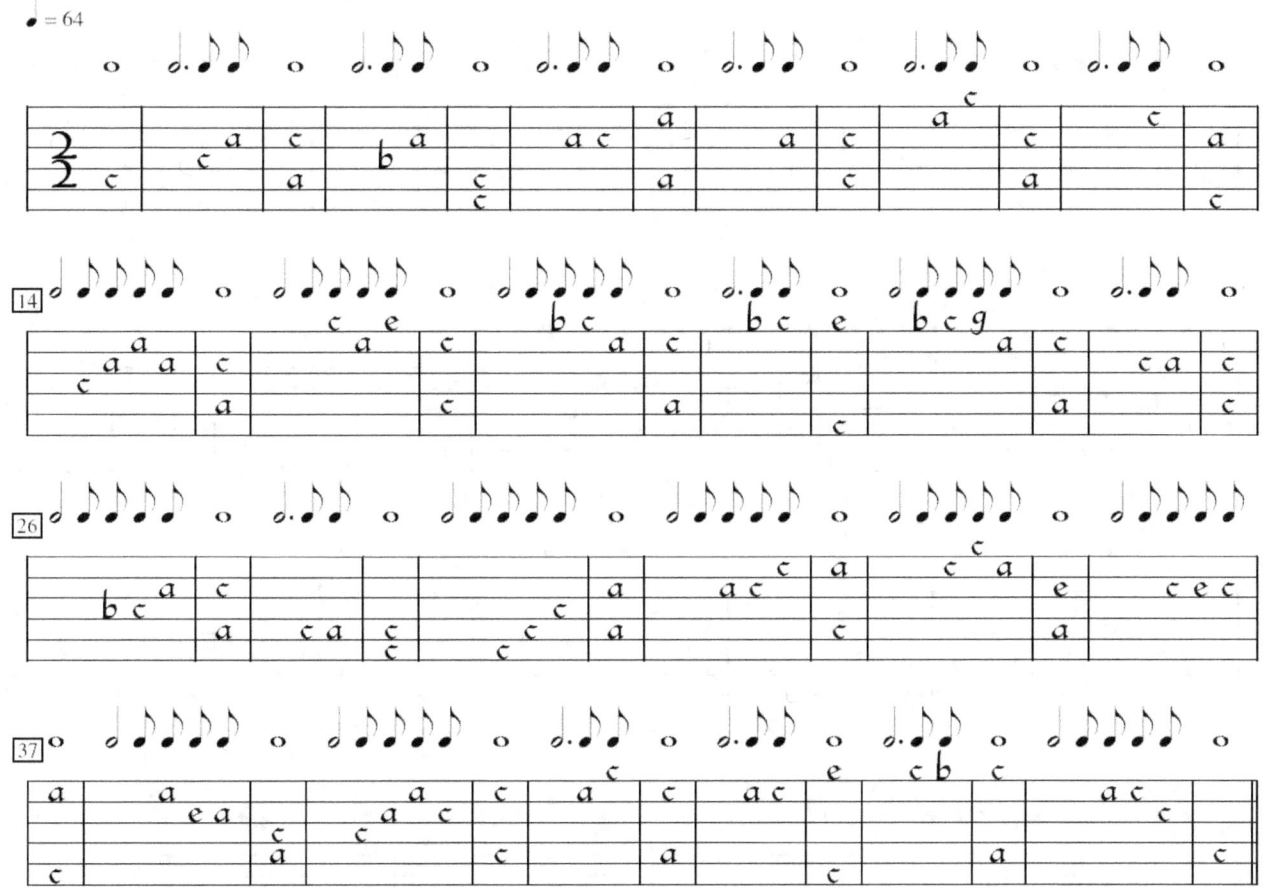

Matthew Leigh Embleton (b1978) — Compositions for Baroque Lute

Op 11 Victoria Park, December 2005 in e-minor (Version 2)

Piano molto e penseroso

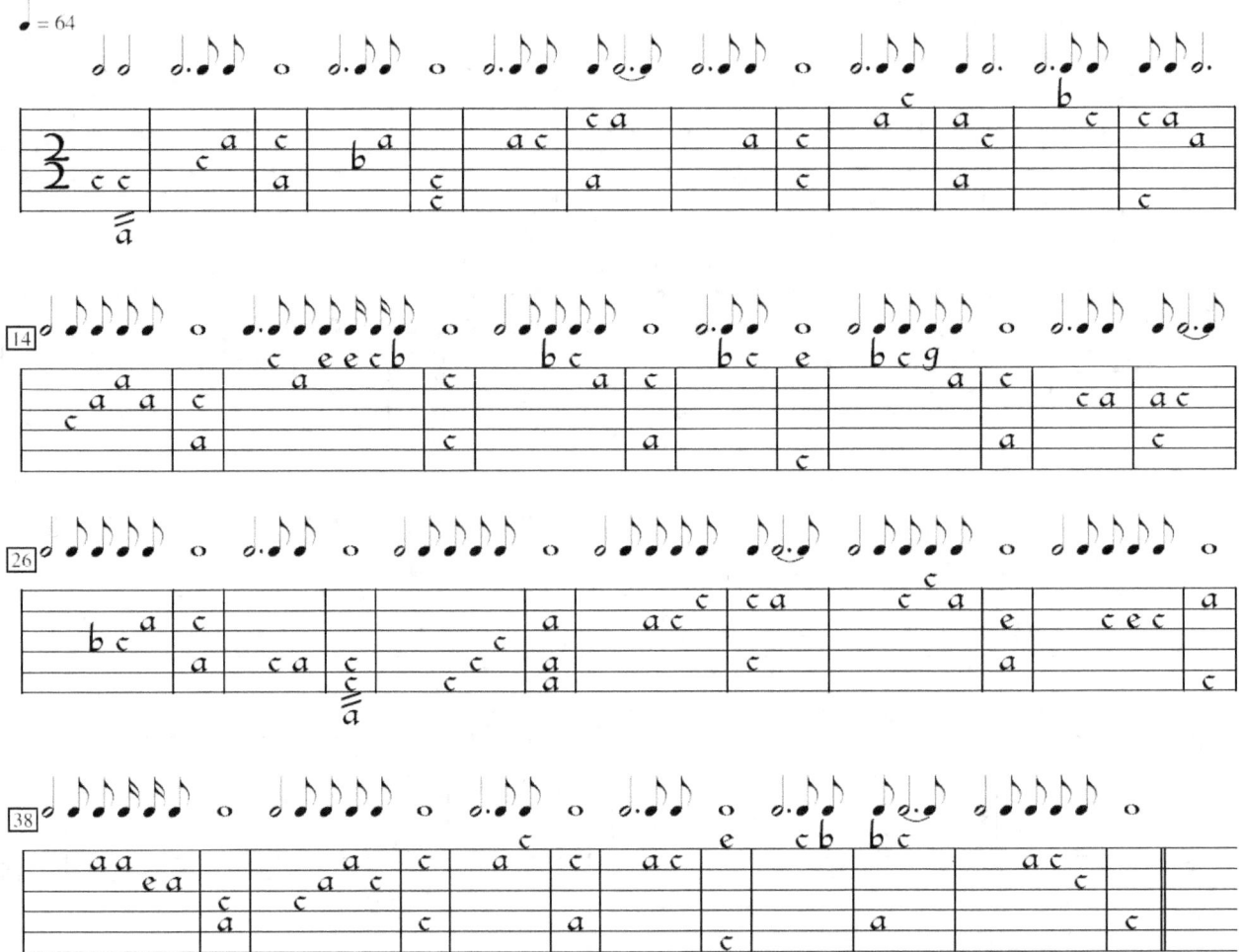

©2012, 2013, 2015, and 2020 Matthew Leigh Embleton

Matthew Leigh Embleton (b1978) — Compositions for Baroque Lute

Op 12 Late Night Sky in g-minor

Piano molto e penseroso

©2012, 2013, 2015, and 2020 Matthew Leigh Embleton

Matthew Leigh Embleton (b1978) — Compositions for Baroque Lute

Op 13 Introduction in g-minor

Piano molto e cantabile

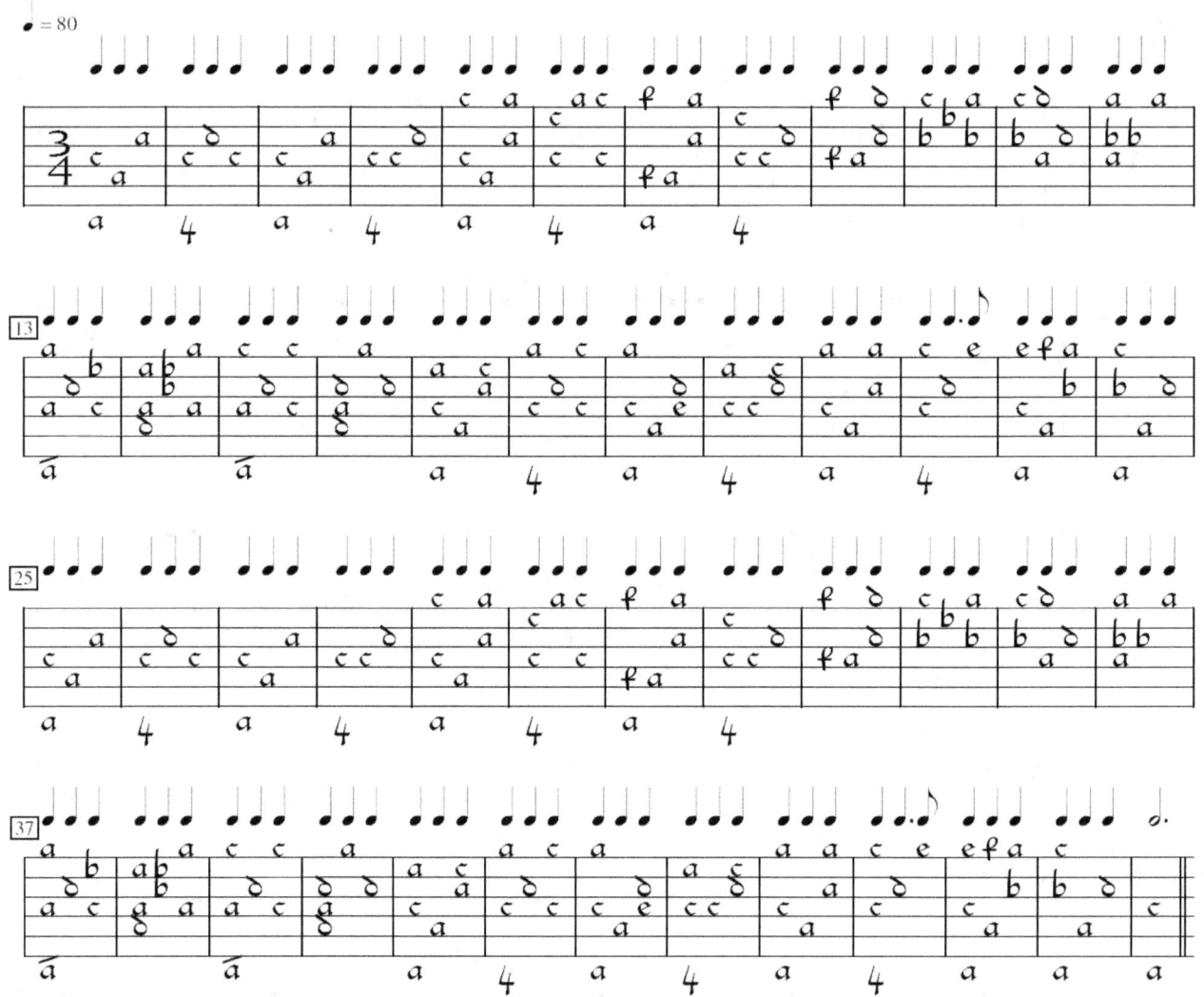

©2012, 2013, 2015, and 2020 Matthew Leigh Embleton

www.ingramcontent.com/pod-product-compliance
Lightning Source LLC
Chambersburg PA
CBHW051427070526
44584CB00023B/3619